Witnessing Answered Prayers

God is Faithful!

Brenda G. Frierson

Inspired Forever Books
Dallas, Texas

Witnessing Answered Prayers: God is Faithful!

Copyright © 2020 Brenda G. Frierson

All rights reserved, including the right of reproduction in whole or in part in any form without prior written permission, except in the case of brief quotations embodied in critical reviews and certain other noncommercial uses permitted by copyright law.

Inspired Forever Book Publishing™
"Words with Lasting Impact"
Dallas, Texas
(888) 403-2727
https://inspiredforeverbooks.com

Library of Congress Control Number: 2020911487

ISBN 13: 978-1-948903-35-6

Printed in the United States of America

Author's Note:

The Bible verses used throughout were taken from some of my favorite translations, including the Revised Standard Version Second Edition and the King James Version Holman Red Letter Edition, among others. I hope you find that the verses I've chosen speak to you as they did to me.

Disclaimer: The events, places, and conversations in this memoir have been recreated from memory, and the information in this book is true and complete to the best of the author's knowledge. The chronology of some events has been compressed. When necessary, the names and identifying characteristics of individuals and places have been changed to maintain anonymity. The views and opinions expressed in this book are those of the author and do not necessarily reflect the official policy or position of the publisher, who shall hold no responsibility or liability resulting from the publication of this material.

Table of Contents

Introduction 1
Seeds of Faith 3
Shadow of Hope 5
Healing the Sick 7
He is Without Fail 9
Boundless Conviction 11
Doing God's Work 13
We Complete One Another 15
A Child's Innocence 17
Love Blooms 19
Pennies from Heaven 21
Joyful Noises 23
Repairing the Broken 25
God is Our Provider 27
Peaceful Moments 29
Safety Nets 31
Spiritual Needs 33
We All Have Value 35
Finding Patience 37
A Final Prayer 39
Afterword: Don't Quit 41
About the Author 43

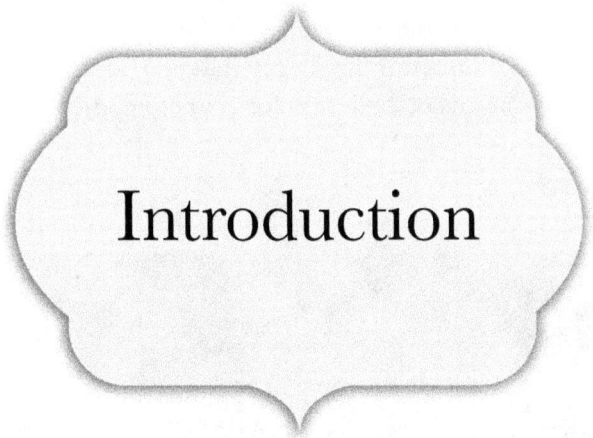

Introduction

If anyone would have told me that God had given me the gift of writing, I would not have believed it. I give God thanks and all the credit for giving me the ability to write this book and humbly submit to His authority when it comes to placing this book into the hands of ordinary people.

I have been on this planet for nearly seven decades, and I have witnessed my share of miracles that can only be explained by supernatural intervention. My love for God continues to grow deeper and deeper over time, and it is difficult to explain it adequately. That's where the stories in this book come in. I hope to inspire you to seek God with all of your heart and trust in Him by showing you the ways in which God has answered my prayers and taken care of my needs. If you let the Holy Scriptures and prayer become part of your daily life, God will take hopeless situations and produce blessings. This may take time; you have to be patient, and you have to have faith.

It is my calling to encourage you to observe that God was and still is at work through the testimonies in this book. God loves each one of us, and He demonstrates this love through so many ways. Let us discover God's truths as we read these stories of *Witnessing Answered Prayers*. Let us begin this journey of prayer together, and let it arouse your faith in God so that He will walk with you throughout your life. I pray that this book will be passed down to generations of believers for years to come.

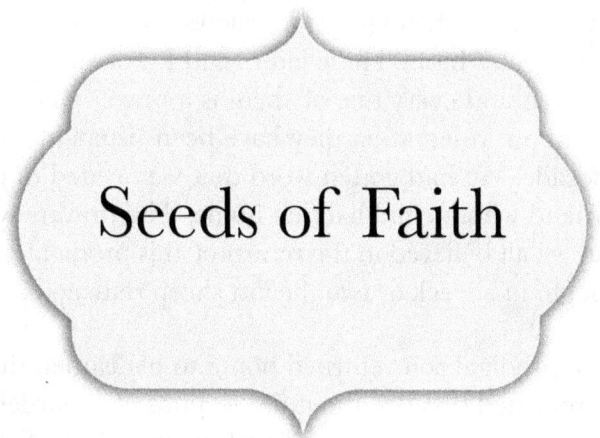

Seeds of Faith

There are extremely difficult times when we must put our full confidence in Him—when helplessness overwhelms us, and our only choice is to trust and believe what we cannot see in the natural.

I have encountered two parents in my life who experienced the devastation of a missing child. I recall the first encounter vividly. It was early one morning—I think around five—and I was sitting with a small prayer group inside a beautiful church when a desperate mother came into the sanctuary crying out for prayer. Her daughter was missing. She had no earthly idea where she was. Our intimate group of intercessors prayed from their hearts for the daughter to return home. In about one week, the mother returned to the church, joyful that her daughter had returned home.

The second time I learned of a child's disappearance, I enlisted the aid of my "round table," as I called it. There was a group of us who would come together in fellowship at my dining room table on a regular basis. These ladies and I remain very close to this day. Each and every one of them is a prayer warrior, and I can say without reservation they have been sisters in Christ for over a decade. We had gotten word that we needed to pray for a close friend whose child had left home. The prayers were fervent, and we all believed in the return of this prodigal son. And sure enough, in a week or two the lost sheep returned home.

Just as the prodigal son returned home to his Father, these two children returned home without the wounds of a hardened life. It gives me confidence to know that God is with us during our dilemmas. The Holy Spirit guides us to the authenticity of God who is well able to deliver our loved ones.

Matthew 17:20

"For I say to you, if you have faith as a grain of a mustard seed, you will say to this mountain, Move from here to there, and it will move; and nothing will be impossible to you."

Shadow of Hope

In our darkest moments, God provides a light to guide us. And if we follow that light, we will know His love.

The bus was running late one evening, and when I arrived at my child's daycare center, it had already closed for the evening. Like any mother would be, I was frantic. I prayed for God to protect my son and to guide me to my child. Mind you, this was decades before cell phones became commonplace. I knew that a teacher must have taken my child home. In the shadow of my memory, I must have had the director's number to locate my precious loved one.

The Holy Spirit guided me, supernaturally, to the home where my precious son was being cared for by a kind and giving person. I can only describe my journey as following a shadow of hope.

Do you believe in miracles? I do. Miracles are for yesterday, today, and forever.

Psalm 77:14

"You are the God who performs miracles; you display your power among the peoples."

Healing the Sick

God's ability to heal us of physical ailments is profound and true if our faith in Him is deep.

Have you ever heard of the woman in the Bible whose infirmity was an "issue of blood?" I have a deep understanding of her suffering because I had the same infirmity. It was during a time when I had no medical insurance, and my finances were practically dried up. Without the ability to pay, there was no medical facility I could go to. Day by day and month by month, I suffered with this ailment. Through my sickness, I still maintained my scheduled college classes as a student and took care of my personal responsibilities.

Finally, I took a bold leap of faith and attended a revival. The evangelist called for someone with female disorders to pray for.

I looked up, and in my heart I realized that God could heal me. No one laid hands on me, even though there were many people at the altar with me.

Not immediately, but slowly over the next several months, the "issue of blood" stopped completely. No medication, no doctors, nothing. Just Jesus the healer. I went for a physical examination. A few years later, I was told by the nurse that my fifty-year-old body was functioning like that of a woman in her twenties. I believe God can do the impossible!

Mark 5:25-29

"And there was a woman who had a flow of blood for twelve years, and who had suffered much under many physicians, and had spent all she had, and was no better but rather grew worse. For she said, if I touch even his garments, I shall be made well. And immediately the hemorrhage ceased; and she felt in her body that she was healed of her disease."

Mark 5:34

"Jesus said to her, daughter, your Faith has made you well; go in peace, and be healed of your disease."

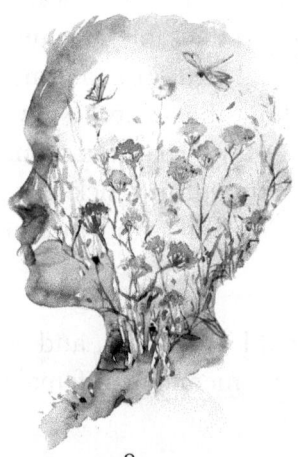

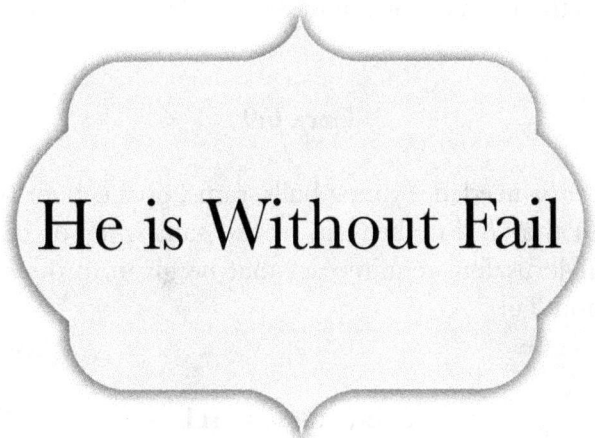

He is Without Fail

Unexpected roadblocks can derail even the steadiest and most confident among us. If we believe that God can do all things without fail, we can stay true to our path and know that He will help us succeed.

It was the spring of 2002, and my college graduation day was approaching. As we were making preparations for the event, I learned that I was nine credit hours short. Panic set in. I realized there wasn't enough funds available to pay for additional courses. I sobbed and cried huge tears. I had worked so hard, and now my dream would have to be put on hold.

God, with His infinite love moved by the Holy Spirit, saw that these classes were paid in full. The university was willing to take care of all costs. God reminded me that He can do all things without fail. My summer of 2002 dreams became a reality. Hallelujah to the Lord of lords and King of kings.

Ezra 6:9

"Whatever is needed—young bulls, rams, or sheep for burnt offerings to the God of heaven, wheat, salt, wine, or oil, as the priests in Jerusalem require—let that be given to them day by day without fail."

Ecclesiastes 9:11

"I returned, and saw under the sun, that the race is not the swift, nor the battle to the strong, neither yet bread to the wise, nor yet riches to men of understanding, nor yet favor to men of skill; but time and chance happeneth to them all."

Boundless Conviction

When our goals at first seem unattainable, we must turn to our faith to empower us. If our belief in Him is unlimited, so are our horizons.

My son had a hope—a dream—for his future, but it was something that seemed unreachable in the natural. Yet he had a powerful desire to pursue his goal anyway.

And suddenly there he was, a young man of fifteen, with a passport and ticket in his hands and suitcases by his side. I'll never forget watching him board that plane on his way to his first mission trip to Peru. Somehow, someway, the Bigness of God had provided the resources. No one can tell me that God cannot provide—that He is not real. God gave this young man favor with ideas, a work ethic, gifts, and a yearning to pursue his true vision. King Jesus lives forever and empowers us to accomplish great things.

Hebrews 11:1

"Now faith is the assurance of things hoped for, the conviction of things not seen."

Doing God's Work

As we reflect upon the ways in which God has used his supernatural ability to bless those who believe in Him, it's natural to wonder how we might do God's work in return. I often ask myself, what is my assignment today from God? The answer to that question is actually right in front of us.

When we look for opportunities to do God's work, we are given a clear view of His Brilliant Light. The door will open to reveal a simple truth: God's road map in the Bible always corresponds with completing the tasks of daily living.

The maintenance on your car, paying bills, cleaning your home, cooking meals, and other priorities are all part of God's plan for us. Yet so often we neglect to understand that God is pleased with us when we perform these simple tasks—ones we might call mundane. The doorway leading to God's work is always open, and when we walk inside, our burdens are lifted because we have obeyed. The joy of the Lord follows, and life can be easier and most of all fulfilling when we accomplish the tasks that are right in front of us.

Revelation 3:20

"Behold, I stand at the door and knock; if anyone hears my voice and opens the door, I will come into him and eat with him, and he with me."

John 14:13

"Whatever you ask in My Name, I will do it, that the Father may be glorified in the Son. If you ask any thing in my name, I will do it.

We Complete One Another

God gave each of us individual gifts—strengths—and intended for us to combine our gifts so that we are stronger as a collective.

Living alone during this season in my life, I have come to realize the significance of family coming together regularly. Each member of a family is important. God in His infinite love supplies to each individual a quality that others can glean from. Yes, one component can bring joy, another mercy, a spirit of peace, and on and on. Meditate on Galatians 5:22-25, and look for the beauty in each person in your life. Let us not look upon family as an old shoe. Ask the Holy Spirit to guide you inwardly to see the gems in one another.

Friends are like red roses. You have heard the saying, "the gift goes on." What a delight when they are alongside us. Friends who have recognized our desire or need to love our mothers beyond life's expectancy. Friends who show up with smiles, gifts, prayers— and just show up to help carry the burden. It is accurate God's children are an expression of His love. Another answer to our prayers.

Galatians 5:22-24-25

"But the fruit of the Spirit is love, joy, peace, longsuffering, gentleness, goodness, faith, meekness, temperance: against there is no law. And they that are Christ's have crucified the flesh with the affections and lusts. If we live in the Spirit, let us also walk in the Spirit."

A Child's Innocence

It's easy to get caught up in our everyday routines. Days start to look alike, and we stop expecting that anything special might happen.

The day began like any typical day at work—one that we all take for granted. On that particular day, I was performing my duties as a substitute teacher, and I received an unexpected, treasured gift.

A precious student I had never seen before presented me with the valuable prize of a teddy bear embroidered with the words "#1 Teacher." The student wanted me to know that it was her choice who should receive it. This sweet young student would not permit me to leave it with her regular instructor. "No," she said. "Mama said I could give it to anyone I wanted to."

It was a delight to see how God used an innocent child to remind me of His unconditional love in an innocent and authentic way. I believe we can all learn lessons from the sincerity of children.

Matthew 18:3-4

"Truly, (Jesus) I say to you, unless you turn and become like children, you will never enter the kingdom of heaven. Whoever humbles himself like this child, he is the greatest in the kingdom of heaven."

Love Blooms

Sometimes the best surprises are those that come from the unknown.

October is a lovely time of year. The fall brings an abundance of breathtaking colors, and on one particular day, I'd had a secret conversation with God in my heart. My desire was for a bouquet of flowers so that I might bring the beautiful colors of autumn into my home.

As I approached my house after work, there were beautiful flowers sitting on my front porch! There was no card attached to the colorful bouquet. The Word is alive! God truly gives you the "desire of your heart." My heavenly loving Father speaks in many ways. He loves me, and He loves you too. What a life to live unspeakable love beyond measure.

Psalm 10:17:

"Lord thou have heard the desire of the humble: thou wilt prepare their hearts, thou wilt cause thine ear to hear."

Pennies from Heaven

Stepping out on faith alone takes real courage when the facts of our circumstances make something seem impossible

It was one of those summers when my income was at the bare minimum. In my heart, I knew that the Holy Spirit was nudging me to attend the funeral of a friend I had known for several years. I was waging a battle with my spirit because my car didn't have much gas. I knew it would not be enough to make the forty-five-minute trip to the funeral. I decided the Holy Spirit was prompting me to step out on FAITH and GO.

I prepared myself to take this journey. I attended the funeral, and at my departure I looked at the ground, not knowing if I would make it home. Suddenly, to my amazement, a five dollar bill was on my front bumper. There was not one soul who knew I was penniless. This was another one of God's aha moments. I confidently walked toward my vehicle and knew it was a miracle from God. Thanks to our heavenly Father who lifts us up from our valley experiences.

1 Corinthians 16:13-14

"Keep alert, stand firm in your faith, be courageous, be strong. Let all that you do be done in love."

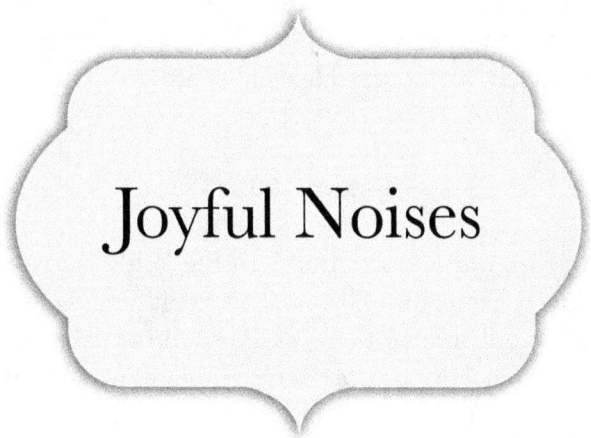

Joyful Noises

When we surrender ourselves completely to God's transformative love, we open ourselves to new experiences and can enrich the lives of those around us.

God loves us so much that extraordinary events can transpire in our lives. One Sunday morning, sitting with the congregation, I began to sing. I lifted my hands, closed my eyes, and worshiped God through the chosen song. Mind you, I am not gifted when it comes to singing. But on that day, my total being was engaged in singing to my Heavenly Father. I had gotten lost in my surroundings and continued to sing.

After the service that morning, I was approached by someone who said to me, "Your singing is beautiful." This has transpired twice during our worship services. I am assured that when we abandon ourselves and focus completely on our Lord and Savior Jesus Christ, Jesus takes over and we become heavenly minded. Remember, the power of the Holy Spirit will operate when we abandon ourselves unto our Heavenly Father.

Psalm 100:1-5

"Make a joyful noise to the Lord, all the lands! Serve the Lord with gladness! Come into His presence with Singing! Know that the Lord is God! It is he that made us, and we are His people. And the sheep of His pasture. Enter His gates with thanksgiving, and His courts with praise! Give thanks to Him, bless His name! For the Lord is good; His steadfast love endures forever, and His faithfulness to all generations."

Repairing the Broken

God never forsakes His children, and our Heavenly Father will never test us with evil.

Appliances and all temporal things have no eternal value, but our Heavenly Father knows that these items can help us complete His work. He can infinitely cause broken things to function again.

The spin cycle on my washing machine had stopped working. I had done my due diligence and contacted a repairman. In the meantime, I simply took my clothes to a nearby laundromat. On the day of the repairman's appointment, I discovered that a few clothes were lying in the washing machine. I prayed, and the machine completed the rinse cycle and the spin cycle worked! When the repairman arrived, I decided not to fix it. I am a believer in miracles, and God knows what He is doing.

Thanks to my beloved Father who causes us to triumph during difficult times and with limited resources. The women in my Bible study group routinely acknowledged specific prayers and everyone would pray for those needs to be met. God answered my prayers, and the leader called me by phone. Her words were, "The Lord wants you to go and pick up your washer." I had looked at a washer earlier in the week and was planning to put it on layaway. But that evening, the Bible study leader and I went together, and she paid for the machine. My God did not test me with evil. My God blessed me.

James 1:13

"Let no one say when he is tempted, I am tempted by God, for God cannot be tempted with evil and He himself tempts no one."

James 1:17

"Every Good endowment and perfect gift is from above, coming down from the Father of lights with whom there is no variation or shadow due to change. Amen!"

God is Our Provider

Divine intervention takes many forms, from the people around us lifting us up during our times of need to the Holy Spirit reassuring us with an overwhelming sense of peace when we are uncertain or afraid.

It was one of those seasons when I desired a change of pace, so I took the opportunity to register for an upcoming conference. I made all the necessary preparations to attend, and had set aside the money I would need to cover gas and my accommodations.

I began my journey with a smile on my face, but as fate would have it, I suddenly noticed that an ambulance was tailing me, as was another car. The driver of the car was trying to get my attention. My car was on fire! Someone had already notified the fire department, so I had amassed my own little convoy of rescue vehicles! The first thought that entered my mind was pull over, and the next thought was that the money I'd set aside for the conference would now go toward repairing the car or buying another one.

Something told me (which I now know was God's Spirit) to stick with my plan. Inwardly, I had a feeling of peace that there would be enough money to pay for my travels and the car. The Holy Spirit gave me a sense of comfort; I was not afraid. I should note that I had paid every bill except my electric bill before leaving for the conference.

It was a memorable conference, and I received an autographed book in a drawing. One of the prophetic speakers called out that someone had a bill to be paid. I have no reservation in telling you the Holy Spirit moved on my behalf. I went alone, to the front, and received the exact amount needed for the bill. God is Jehovah Jireh my provider!

Psalm 91:2

"I will say of the lord, "He is my refuge and my fortress; My God, in Him I will trust."

Peaceful Moments

When we embark upon new journeys—new tests—our fears will subside when we surrender to the Holy Spirit.

The beauty of nature surrounds our lives and is often a source of great comfort to me. In July 2000 when I was around fifty years old, I had moved to a new, completely unfamiliar county. Fear allowed doubts to creep in, and I began to question God.

I was standing on the deck surrounding my home with my head tilted upward, and all I could see was blackness. In that moment of time, my soul felt a silent peace, and rather than blackness, I was filled with a new appreciation for what God was allowing me to see. I've learned to enjoy with deep awe and great pleasure these "God moments." Tests and trials seem to evaporate when the scripture comes alive.

Witnessing Answered Prayers

Psalm 16:11

"Thou dost show me the path of life; in thy right hand are pleasures for evermore."

Safety Nets

In this life, we cannot predict what each day will hold. We must trust that God will give us what we need to get through unpredictable circumstances.

I remember the sheer panic I felt as if it were yesterday. It had rained nonstop the entire day and throughout the night. My husband and I were awakened by a barrage of noises—some were loud voices muffled by the constant rain, and some sounds were mechanical, like vehicles. We looked outside to see rescue workers and neighbors shouting at us to get out of the house. What we saw when we looked out our window wasn't just rain; it was a FLOOD. The water had already surrounded the foundation of the house and was rapidly rising. We had to swim.

I was paralyzed with fear and couldn't move. My husband got our baby boy to safety first and came back to rescue me. I could not swim. Panic overwhelmed me. Stiff and afraid, I could not move. But then, somehow, I did. I started moving through the water as if propelled by an unseen force. I know now without skepticism that God's power pushed me across the rising waters. I believe without a doubt that invisible angels were rescuing me. The rescue workers and others were cheering me on as I reached the safety point.

How many times in our lives have we faced major catastrophes and never realized God provided safety nets for each of us? I give God thanks for saving my life. He loves us beyond measure that the natural mind cannot comprehend.

Jonah 2:1-2

"Then Jonah prayed unto the Lord his God out of the fish's belly. And said, I cried by reason of mine affliction unto the Lord, and He heard me; out of the belly of hell cried I, and He heard my voice."

Spiritual Needs

Occasionally, we are reminded that life's little inconveniences can be blessings in disguise.

When my fourteen-year-old garage door needed a new spring, it turned out to be a blessing in disguise! God handpicked the right person to fix the broken part, and it was a divine moment when I was able to talk briefly with this person. He saw my Bible lying on the kitchen table. He was from another country (Israel) and believed in God, but his belief was that the Messiah had not returned.

I was led by the Lord to write down scriptures from the Old Testament (Torah) that specifically had Jesus in them. I did exactly what my heart prompted me to do.

The repairman returned the following week and replaced the spring in the garage door. I had told him during our first visit that "I hope he could do a good job." He had promptly reassured me, "I am going to do a great job replacing the spring." He fixed the garage door, and when he left that day I gave him the scriptures. I knew that God was not only meeting my personal needs but also my spiritual needs. I had already prayed that God would send the right person. God and I in agreement prayed that this man would be enlightened to the truth. God always has our day orchestrated if we will allow it.

1 Corinthians 2:7

"So then neither is he that plant anything, he that water, but God that giveth the increase."

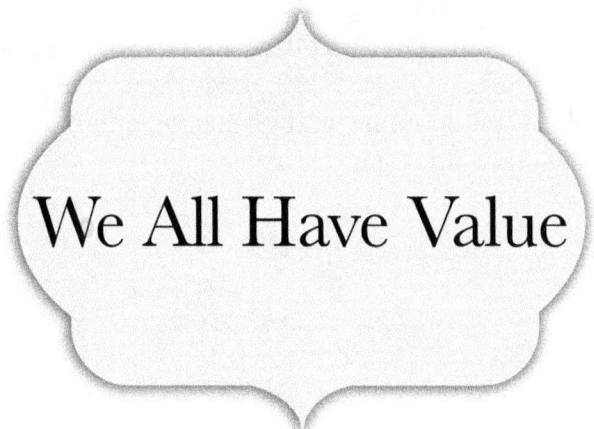

We All Have Value

It's amazing how others can see the potential in us that we cannot see ourselves. We are all valuable to God, and it is important that we recognize the value in each other.

Sometimes, on an ordinary, routine day, the extraordinary happens! During my years attending a local community college, I would often stop by the office of an admissions worker to say hello before entering the classroom. On one particular day, the admissions worker wanted to know if I would be willing to talk about my experiences as a student during an event for students entering college for the first time. I was delighted and knew God had prompted this special moment. God sees us and knows our potential because He created each one of us with significance.

Jeremiah 29:11-12:

"For I know the thoughts that I think toward you, said the Lord, thoughts of peace, and not of evil, to give you an expected end. Then shall ye call upon me, and ye shall go and pray unto me, and I will hearken unto you."

Finding Patience

The plans that God has for our lives are good plans. We must remain patient while we allow God's perfect will to unfold.

Journaling has always been one of my favorite pastimes, even as a young girl. In 1974 when I was twenty-two years old, I decided to organize my thoughts and submit an article to our local newspaper. To my amazement, the newspaper chose to publish it! I was excited because my heavenly Father allowed this dream to surface. To God be the glory, for He has done great things. Lord, you are faithful to your promises.

James 1:2-8

"My brethren, count it all joy when you fall into various trials, knowing that the testing of your faith produces patience. But let patience have its perfect work, that you may be perfect and complete, lacking nothing."

A Final Prayer

The Word of God teaches us about faith and love. We know that God's love cannot be contained. The song "Trust and Obey" by Don Moen triggers or radiates flashes of His love for mankind. As I walked through each one of these circumstances that I have described for you in this book, I gained an understanding of how much Jesus loves us all. His abundance of love cannot be compared to anyone else's.

By faith, a young child takes one tiny step. We can compare ourselves to the infant— stumbling yet not giving up—determined to reach out in faith and being courageous in learning how to walk.

At times as faith began to take root in my life, I knew it was God who took my hand courageously and gently soothed my deepest pain and hardship, and gave me the love I desperately needed. When we are truly desperate for God to occupy our lives, we should encourage and labor in prayer for others so that they will see their lives blessed in phenomenal ways.

I'll leave you with a prayer that each one of us will earnestly know God in His character and that we will learn to possess many of Jesus's attributes. Our natural bodies are constantly decaying. It is only the Holy Spirit who empowers us to triumph in this walk with God. Pray as you begin to see through spiritual eyes a journey that brings faith and love for God in an ordinary life that activates a supernatural God that is glorified daily.

> "When we walk with the Lord in the light of His Word,
> What a glory He sheds on our way;
> While we do His good will, He abides with us still,
> And with all who will trust and obey."
>
> **~ From the hymn "Trust and Obey"**

When we walk with the Lord in the light of His Word,

What a glory He sheds on our way...

Afterword: Don't Quit

I come to encourage you to continue in the faith! God is your deliverer. He will see you through every sickness, trial, distress, and trying circumstance. God doesn't want you to give up. Continue, my friend, to hold on to God's hand and never lose heart no matter what besets and grips you.

The patriots of old had to trust God for every painful situation they faced. King David as a young boy had to trust God. You know the story: David went out to kill the giant, Goliath. (1 Samuel 17:37) David said, "The Lord who delivered me out of the paw of the lion and out of the bear. He will deliver me out of the hand of this Philistine." David was delivered out of the clutches of Goliath.

Deborah, a prophetess and judge, served Israel. (Judges 4:9) Deborah said to Barak. "I will go with thee: notwithstanding the journey that you take shall not be for your honor: for the Lord Jehovah shall see Sisera into the hand of a woman." If Deborah had not followed God's command, I believe Israel would have continued to be in bondage of a wicked king. Faith steered her to obey God.

Jesus will never leave or abandoned his children. We must speak to our intellect: *I will not quit. God is with me!*

About the Author

Brenda Gale Frierson was born in Nashville, Tennessee. She is a proud mother to two sons who also reside in Tennessee. Brenda knows that God is faithful! She believes that life is a journey, and we have a beginning and a final destiny best served if we use our personal gifts to inspire others.

www.ingramcontent.com/pod-product-compliance
Lightning Source LLC
Chambersburg PA
CBHW061517040426
42450CB00008B/1657